AF399819

CONSTRUCTIVE FEEDBACK

The essentials of giving and receiving constructive criticism

Written by Véronique Bronckart
Translated by Carly Probert

CONSTRUCTIVE FEEDBACK

- **Problem:** accepting criticism is not always easy, and nor is giving criticism without offending or upsetting the other person. What techniques can be used to deliver effective and constructive feedback? How can you take advantage of the feedback you receive?
- **Uses:** feedback is essential for both you and your colleagues, as it allows you to change, maintain or correct your behaviour in order to achieve your goals.
- **Professional context:** team management, interpersonal skills, personal development.
- **FAQs:**
  - What is feedback?
  - When should I give feedback?
  - What tone should I use to ensure that my feedback will be taken on board?
  - What steps are involved?
  - What is the difference between feedback and judgement?

- What mistakes should be avoided?
- I find it difficult to accept criticism. How can I make sure that I take feedback well?
- The person involved is very sensitive. How can I make sure that they accept my feedback?
- How can I ensure that my feedback has been effective?
- Can anything be discussed when giving feedback?

Given the increasing importance of efficiency and progress in the modern business world, feedback is essential to make us aware of our strengths, our weaknesses and any areas for improvement. But if feedback is not common practice in your company, how can you explain to an employee or colleague that they need to change their attitude or working methods without hurting them? How can you congratulate a person without them resting on their laurels in the future? Similarly, how can you constructively accept criticism from other people? But before you make constructive feedback a part of your work, you will need to understand exactly what it is and how to deliver it.

In just 50 minutes, this guide will teach you the golden rules of giving and receiving constructive feedback so that you can use it to motivate employees and boost results. Receiving feedback on their performance allows employees to improve and offers development opportunities, so take on board all of our tips to make the most of this valuable management tool.

EFFECTIVE FEEDBACK: THE BASICS

WHAT DOES FEEDBACK INVOLVE?

What is feedback?

TERMINOLOGY

The *Merriam-Webster Learner's Dictionary* defines feedback as "helpful information or criticism that is given to someone to say what can be done to improve a performance, product, etc.". It highlights strengths, weaknesses and potential areas for improvement.

Feedback is an evaluation of a completed project or an action performed at a given time which is transmitted to an individual or a group of people. The purpose of this exchange is to reinforce positive behaviours or to allow the people involved to modify their approach in future.

Feedback is designed to allow managers to show their appreciation to an employee or team: it is an opportunity to congratulate people on their work. There are two ways to do this:

- Verbally, by clearly expressing your opinion. This is called direct feedback.
- Non-verbally, through a gesture or silence. This indirect feedback shows the other person that they are on the right track.

For feedback to be effective, it must be neutral and be transmitted on a regular basis as soon as possible after the relevant behaviour. Ideally, it should be given face to face, in a quiet place. It is not about judging or trying to change the other person, as this risks upsetting them or putting them on the defensive. Remember that feedback is not synonymous with criticism or punishment: rather than lashing out over something you are unhappy about, your aim should be to make the employee aware of their mistakes, any areas for improvement and your expectations for them.

Feedback always focuses on the facts in order to help the individual to improve their skills, behaviour and performance. It must be accompanied by clear, precise objectives so that the person understands why they need to change their approach or work on their skills in a particular area.

The four types of feedback

We can distinguish four types of feedback, which all have different effects. Reinforcing and constructive feedback are recommended, while flattering and provocative feedback should be avoided.

- **Reinforcing feedback** (positive and specific): the person's actions are complimented and they are encouraged to keep going. This type of feedback increases self-esteem and seeks to maintain the person's current behaviour.

  > **Example**
  > "Luke, I appreciate you prioritising this task. It should be finalised this week, and without your cooperation this wouldn't be possible! Keep taking initiatives like this."

- **Constructive or corrective feedback** (negative and specific): the person's actions are criticised in a positive way so that they can be adjusted. This preserves the individual's self-esteem and seeks to improve behaviour.

> **Example**
> "Ellie, I've noticed that you've arrived late three times this month. You've been about 10 to 15 minutes late each time; I think you can easily find a solution to address this."

- **Flattering feedback** (positive and non-specific): this is issued at any time and without any specific reason. It engenders mistrust and reduces self-esteem, and the individual may feel that they owe their manager something.

> **Example**
> "Tom, you're the best! I know I can always count on you."

- **Provocative feedback** (negative and non-specific): this is more of a judgement than feedback. It greatly reduces self-esteem and can result in mental blocks.

> **Example**
> "I always said I couldn't trust you and you've proved me right, yet again. You are useless!"

	Reinforcing feedback +	Corrective or constructive feedback -
On their actions	"I'm happy that you took charge of this task and that you take initiative, this helps us a lot." "Your contribution during the meeting yesterday was very effective, it allowed us to move forward with the task." "I'm very happy with the way you wrote this report, it is very clear and precise."	"I noticed that you often arrive late." "I noticed that your files are not organised well." "Your project report is incomplete and lacks precision."

	Reinforcing feedback +	Corrective or constructive feedback -
On their personality	"I appreciate your skills in this area." "Your reaction this morning to this particular case was appropriate and allowed us to avoid a disaster." "Even though I don't totally agree, your opinion on this file is interesting."	Corrective feedback is never given about the person.

	Flattering feedback +	Provocative feedback -
On their actions	"Your work is great!" "As usual, you managed the situation very well!" "Your files are always so organised."	"Your contribution made the situation worse, it did no good!" "Your report is really bad." "Your office is a complete pigsty!"
On their personality	"You're so brave!" "Your efficiency is amazing!" "You're the ideal colleague!"	"You're useless!" "Your behaviour is dreadful." "You have been nothing but a disaster for this company."

The effectiveness of feedback

Feedback is an essential tool if we want to make progressive adjustments to improve and achieve our objectives. It is a tool for communicating, measuring and monitoring performance, as it lets individuals know where they stand and whether or not they are dealing with a particular situation effectively. It also highlights areas for improvement.

To deliver feedback effectively, it is essential to:

- Notify the person in advance to prepare them for your feedback.
- Stick to the facts and describe the actions and/or behaviour you have observed.
- Explain the consequences of this.
- If you are giving reinforcing feedback, ask the person to keep going as they are. This will ensure that they maintain the same approach.
- If you are giving constructive feedback, do not force them to make changes, but ask them to find a solution themselves.

Positive feedback meets the employee's self-esteem and belonging needs, which will motivate them to keep going on the right track. Maslow's hierarchy of needs (developed by the American psychologist Abraham Maslow, 1908-1970) demonstrates that our needs are prioritised according to their importance. Following this logic, the needs at the bottom of the pyramid must be met before the higher needs can be satisfied.

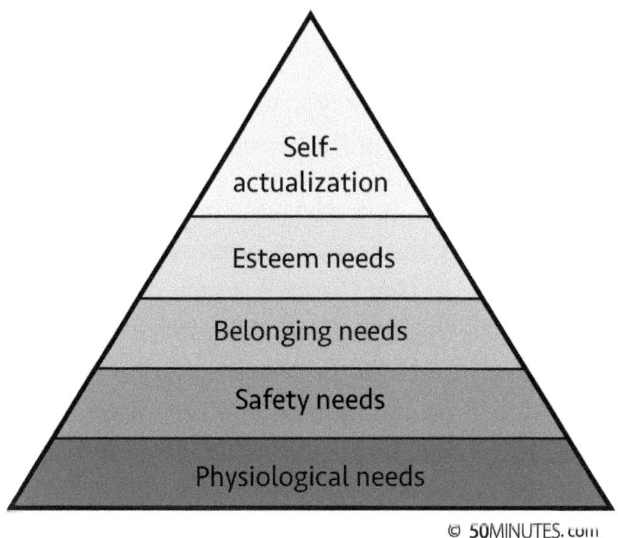

© 50MINUTES.com

The recognition and praise of an employee's skills is a powerful motivating force. Without this recognition, the individual feels less of a need to make an effort and gradually loses their motivation. On the other hand, if their efforts are clearly identified and noted, they will see that hard work pays off and will want to continue on the same path.

THE ART OF GIVING CONSTRUCTIVE FEEDBACK

Preparation

Before giving feedback, you will need to agree on a suitable time and place to deliver it.

- **The right time.** It is advisable to begin the discussion with the relevant employees as soon as possible, so that the exchange is meaningful and has the desired effect. If feedback is delivered three months later, there is a good chance that it will be ineffective: your employee will probably have forgotten what they did and will not understand your explanations.
- **The right place.** It is also very important to choose a suitable location. It is both difficult for you and unpleasant for the other person to receive feedback during a meal with colleagues or by the coffee machine during your break. Plan a meeting with the person at a specific time in a neutral location, and tell them in advance so that they are not taken unawares.

Make sure that the feedback comes from you directly: if you ask a team leader or colleague to deliver it, they may distort your message or even not pass it on at all. Avoid relying on hearsay and make sure that you are delivering your feedback to the right person.

<u>THINGS TO AVOID</u>

- Giving feedback in front of a group of people who are not involved in the matter at hand.
- Waiting for the annual performance review to deliver feedback.
- Formulating feedback too hastily, without taking the time to explain or listen to your employee.

Explaining the situation

The first step in giving effective feedback is to clearly establish the context. You will need to give your employee a clear, concrete reminder of the situation in which the behaviour or action was observed. Make sure that they remember and understand what you are talking about.

If you say "This Monday afternoon, during the

meeting with the supplier, I found that...", the employee can immediately identify what you are referring to and will listen carefully. However, if you start with "During the meeting, I found that...", they will have to think to try to recall the meeting you are referring to and will only be half-listening to what you say.

Adopting the right attitude

Feedback always focuses on analysing a behaviour or action and does not carry a judgement. Be as neutral and empathetic as possible. Do not show your dissatisfaction in an impulsive or aggressive way, as this may make the situation worse. If you share your point of view objectively and base your comments on the facts, your employee will be more receptive to the feedback. Using purely descriptive language will also make the conversation easier.

Make your employee feel at ease by showing them that you want to help them, not punish them. Feedback should be a two-way street: you need to listen and let the employee speak and give their explanations, opinions and feelings on the situation.

Finally, try to find concrete and realistic avenues for improvement together. If you promote exchange and involve your employee, they will feel less threatened and become aware of the changes needed. If you say "For some time, I've noticed that your files are not organised and are getting lost. Could you tell me what you intend to do to fix this?", the person will be more receptive and likely to change their behaviour than if you say "Your files are a mess, it's driving me crazy!".

Delivering the message

Rather than delivering your feedback out of the blue, start with a short introduction like "Can I discuss something with you?" to give the person an idea of what is coming.

Your message should be short, clear and precise. Avoid giving overly long explanations or discussing other similar experiences you have had. Remember the facts and deliver them calmly using simple and precise words. Your main aim should be to describe the behaviour observed (whether it is positive or negative) and its consequences.

Make sure that the employee has understood your message and there is no room for misunderstanding. End your speech by:

- encouraging them, in the case of constructive feedback;
- praising them, in the case of reinforcing feedback.

Setting a clear goal

Explain the impact of the person's behaviour on you or the company. Your aim here is not to make them feel guilty, but to make them aware of their actions and their consequences so that they can improve. Set a clear goal and make sure that your employee has understood your expectations, otherwise they may not grasp the need for change. Give them the opportunity to express any suggestions for improvement. If they do not have any ideas, discuss potential new approaches together and set objectives. At the end of the meeting, show them that they have your complete support.

Example
"From now on, you should taste your sauce before serving it to make sure it isn't too salty.

Monitoring developments

After delivering your feedback, you will need to monitor your employee's behaviour over the long term. It is likely that they will need time to truly improve, so be patient. If you cannot see any improvement after the meeting, check that the employee has understood your message and, if necessary, ask them again to make improvements.

TIP FOR EMPLOYERS

It has been shown that employers mainly use feedback to criticise. However, it is just as important to congratulate employees when they deserve it and encourage them to stay on track.

Mistakes to avoid

It is not easy to successfully transmit effective, productive and well-received feedback. We are often worried that we will not express ourselves clearly and that our comments may be misinterpreted and seen as a rebuke. We are also afraid of saying things we might later regret and which could damage our working relationships.

Mistake	**Passing judgement:** The most common error is passing judgement on the individual, instead of their actions. This becomes more of a criticism (non-constructive). By expressing your thoughts too directly and impulsively, you risk making your employee defensive. They may consider your feedback as a personal attack, they will feel obliged to justify themselves and waste their energy defending themselves. This greatly reduces the chances of opening up a positive and constructive discussion.
What not to say	"You should learn to work in a team!" "You don't know how to work in a team!"
What you should say	"The way you work in a team is not ideal, you should try to improve this."

Mistake	**Being too indirect:** If you formulate your points in an interrogative manner, you risk being misinterpreted by your employee. They may react badly or simply not take in what you are saying.
What not to say	"Do you think you could be more attentive and reactive next time?"
What you should say	"I hope that you will be more attentive and reactive next time."

Mistake	**Being too vague:** Your employee will not understand why you are delivering the information at this exact time or what you expect of them. If you want the person to continue being effective, you should explain to them clearly why they have pleased you, what has been positive and which behaviour you want to continue.
What not to say	"You've really proved yourself." "You did excellent work on the Peters file."
What you should say	"On this particular case from this morning, you did really good work." "The corrections you made on the Peters file were very constructive. They allowed us to avoid administrative problems in the future."

Mistake	**Taking too long:** It is important to limit the length of your feedback meeting. It is useless to start comparing the situation with your personal experience, giving lots of advice or trying to solve multiple problems at once. Do not overload your employee with excess information, as they will find it difficult to take it all in and no progress will be made.
What not to say	"Although I know it is not always clear how to face this type of situation, I think that the behaviour of certain members of the team is not always appropriate and this leads to problems...I myself remember when..."
What you should say	"Paul and Mark's behaviour during yesterday's crisis meeting was not appropriate and caused problems within the company." (You can develop this statement by explaining why.)

Mistake	**Using sarcasm:** If you use it with your colleague who arrives late to a meeting it will have no positive effects, as they will not realise the reason for your behaviour. This type of feedback is generally given when a situation is difficult to face and unsaid words pass between people.
What not to say	"Right on time, as always!"
What you should say	"I hope you will arrive on time for meetings. It is a sign of respect towards your colleagues and clients." (Said after the meeting has finished.)

Mistake	**Threatening:** Telling someone that their position is at stake will not encourage them to improve their behaviour, as they will not understand the facts you are communicating. On the contrary, this may reduce their motivation and make the situation worse.
What not to say	"With behaviour like that, you'll never last in our company."
What you should say	"It would be a good idea to make some changes to your behaviour. This would help you to grow within the company."

Mistake	**Giving negative criticism in between two positive comments:** This stems from good intentions to start and finish feedback on a positive note in order to reassure your employee. However, your message will not be welcomed and understood the way you want it to be. In fact, your employee will interpret it as a move on your part to make a negative comment and will not retain any aspect of your message. Saying things clearly and directly is the best solution.
What not to say	"I know that you are someone I can count on, but I was disappointed with your efficiency last week, even though I know you did all you could to make sure everything was perfect."
What you should say	"Your efficiency last week disappointed me."

Mistake	**Generalising:** If you use terms such as "always" or "never", your employee will become defensive as they will think of all the times when they did not do what you are talking about.
What not to say	"You should never turn your back on clients."
What you should say	"When you call a colleague to ask for something for a client, don't turn your back, this may be taken as a sign of disrespect."

Mistake	**Basing your comments on the opinions of others:** Your employee will be disconcerted by your comments if they do not come from you. They will try to identify which colleagues have given you these opinions. They will become defensive, which means that they will not concentrate on what you are saying and may not hear your message.
What not to say	"I've heard that you didn't participate in the last meeting constructively."
What you should say	"Reading your report, it seems to me that you didn't participate very constructively in the last meeting."

Mistake		**Talking about their private life:** If you analyse the current situation of your employee or the psychological reasons for their behaviour, you risk incorrectly identifying the source of their problems. It is definitely not productive to pry into the private life of your employee. On the contrary, this may result in bitterness towards you and your feedback.
What not to say		"Your divorce should not have an impact on the efficiency of your work."
What you should say		"I've noticed a drop in efficiency In your work recently."

THE ART OF RECEIVING AND ACCEPTING FEEDBACK

Although we tend to hold the person giving the feedback responsible for its effectiveness, it is equally important that the person receiving it is ready to listen, understand and accept it. Few people handle criticism well, often because of a lack of self-confidence. For the conversation to be as constructive as possible, the recipient must keep an open mind and listen actively.

Tips

- Be receptive and open to accepting remarks positively. Avoid rushing to judgement or taking the criticism personally. Concentrate on what is being said and give the person time to finish what they have to say.
- Listen carefully to understand the bigger picture, before focusing on specifics and areas for improvement.
- There is no need to get defensive or try to justify everything. Even if you do not completely agree with the feedback you have received, it is best to specify only the information you feel is relevant. This will prevent the conversation from descending into an attempt to apportion blame.
- Make sure you have understood everything. If necessary, ask for clarification to prevent any

misunderstandings. The person giving you the feedback will appreciate the seriousness with which you are approaching the situation.

- If the criticism is unjustified, stay calm. Try to explain your point of view without overreacting.
- To avoid losing your temper, take a step back and explain that you need some time to think things over.
- Even if you feel attacked during the feedback, do not lash out, as this will only make things worse. Try to understand where your manager is coming from. Even if they are wrong about some things, you probably still have some flaws to work on.
- If you are naturally sensitive, keep in mind that feedback is given to help you improve and make progress. Receiving criticism does not mean that you have failed, but rather that you have the potential to go further.

The Johari window

Feedback has many benefits, including greater self-awareness. Indeed, we have only a partial view of ourselves, but the people around us can help us to complete the picture. Their comments will give you a better idea of your flaws and qualities, and over the long term this will increase your self-confidence.

The Johari window, which was developed in 1955 by the American psychologists Joseph Luft (1916-2014) and Harrington Ingham (1914-1995), is a tool to illustrate the knowledge we have of ourselves and the knowledge others have of us.

Open zone Known by you and others	**Blind zone** Known only by others
Hidden zone Known only by you	**Unknown zone** Unknown by you and others (the subconscious)

By accepting feedback on your blind spots, you will discover weaknesses (and strengths) that you had perhaps not been aware of until now and that you can overcome (or strengthen) in order to progress. You will also be able to enlarge the public area, which will promote communication with others.

TIP FOR EMPLOYEES

Listen carefully to what you are told, and view feedback as an opportunity to improve rather than a personal attack.

TOP TIPS

THE 12 GOLDEN RULES

- Create a climate of trust by reassuring the other person. Make them understand that the purpose of the feedback is to help, not to punish.
- Remain neutral and do not pass judgement.
- Avoid negativity and aggression.
- Proceed in stages: introduction, statement of the facts, discussion, development of solutions.
- Adjust your feedback depending on the employee and their personality.
- Avoid information overload – stick to the essentials!
- Deliver a clear and precise message.
- Check that the message and its purpose are understood.
- Focus on actions or facts, not the individual's personality.
- Listen to and connect with the other person.
- Agree on improvements together.

- End on a positive note by encouraging your employee and reassuring them that you trust them to find solutions.

FAQS

WHAT IS FEEDBACK?

Feedback is the evaluation of person's behaviour or actions, issued with the purpose of encouraging them to change or maintain their current approach. Feedback is non-judgemental. It can be positive or negative (as long as the criticism is constructive) and verbal or non-verbal.

WHEN SHOULD I GIVE FEEDBACK?

Feedback should be given as soon as possible after the event for greater effectiveness. If you give feedback weeks later, your employee might not remember some of the details and will not understand why you are bringing them up now. There is no need to wait for an exceptional event to give feedback: it is also a great tool for recognition and can be given at any time to encourage your employees.

WHAT TONE SHOULD I USE TO ENSURE THAT MY FEEDBACK WILL BE TAKEN ON BOARD?

Adopt a neutral but empathetic tone. If you are too familiar, your employee might not take your comments seriously. That being said, if you are too hard on them, they may react negatively and be less receptive to your comments.

WHAT STEPS ARE INVOLVED?

In order for your feedback to be constructive, you need to prepare: warn the other person in advance and arrange a time to talk to them. During the conversation, create an environment of trust, explain the facts clearly, and ask them for their opinion and their feelings to make them feel involved. Finally, try to find solutions for improvement together. Do not forget to reassure your employee: feedback should not be a source of discomfort or fear.

WHAT IS THE DIFFERENCE BETWEEN FEEDBACK AND JUDGEMENT?

Feedback is based on actions or behaviour rather than the individual's personality. It must not have a negative effect on their self-esteem, self-confidence, motivation or effectiveness. The purpose of feedback is to encourage the recipient to keep improving. A judgement is an opinion based on someone or something, and is not necessarily justified.

WHAT MISTAKES SHOULD BE AVOIDED?

- Being aggressive or judgemental may make the situation worse.
- Feedback should be carried out privately, away from people who are not involved in the matter at hand.
- Do not deliver a monologue, preventing the speaker from contributing and expressing their opinion or feelings. Remember that feedback should be constructive and non-punitive. It is important to be as clear as possible to avoid potential misunderstandings.

- Do not base your comments on other people's observations or on generalities. Your feedback should be precise and supported by irrefutable facts.

I FIND IT DIFFICULT TO ACCEPT CRITICISM. HOW CAN I MAKE SURE THAT I TAKE FEEDBACK WELL?

To receive feedback positively, be receptive and open-minded, and listen carefully to what the other person is trying to say. Do not be defensive, as this will stop you from learning from the experience. If necessary, you can provide some explanations and ask for clarification of the facts.

THE PERSON INVOLVED IS VERY SENSITIVE. HOW CAN I MAKE SURE THAT THEY ACCEPT MY FEEDBACK?

If the other person is naturally sensitive, it is best to reassure them and put them at ease by adopting a neutral but empathetic tone. Remind them that this is not a negative criticism or a judgement, but a constructive comment that will enable them to improve. Feedback will make them aware of their strengths, their weaknesses and any areas for improvement. Clearly explain the impact of their behaviour and your expectations, and let them express their feelings so that they feel heard and understood. Ask them to suggest areas for improvement. If they think of the solution themselves, they will be more willing to accept it.

HOW CAN I ENSURE THAT MY FEEDBACK HAS BEEN EFFECTIVE?

Monitoring your employee's behaviour after you have agreed on changes together is essential to ensure that they make the necessary adjustments. The results of feedback are most visible over the long term.

CAN ANYTHING BE DISCUSSED WHEN GIVING FEEDBACK?

Some subjects are off limits during feedback. For example, you should avoid talking about your employee's personal life or mental health, as this could engender resentment and make the situation worse. Furthermore, focusing too much on the other person's private life may lead you to draw the wrong conclusions.

OVER TO YOU

EXERCISE 1

Read and analyse the following feedback:

> **Employer**: Hi Paul, could you come into my office? I have something I want to discuss with you.
> **Employee**: Hello Sir, yes, of course... is there a problem?
> **Employer**: I heard that you made an inappropriate comment at the marketing meeting. I hope that doesn't happen again!
> **Employee**: Which comment are you referring to?
> **Employer**: Your comments on the new concept introduced by our colleagues in Paris.
> **Employee**: I just wanted to let them know that there were some mistakes...
> **Employer**: The mistake you made was the way you delivered the criticism! You've ruined our working relationship with the French team! I'm really not happy about that. Don't let it happen again. You may leave and return to your work.

- What type of feedback is this?
- Is it effective feedback? Explain your answer.

- Is the employer's attitude appropriate and justified? Explain your answer.
- Does the feedback end on a positive note?
- What changes would you make so that the feedback is constructive?

EXERCISE 2

After sharing feedback with one of your employees, analyse your exchange by completing the table below:

	Analysis	To improve
Choice of location Neutral or not?		
Choice of time • How long after the event occurred? • What time of day?		
Situation Brief description of the reason and development of the feedback		
Behaviour Tone and attitude adopted		
Message • Was it clear? • Short? • Precise? • Understood?		
Impact • Was it expressed? • What are the objectives? • What are the points for improvement?		

	Analysis	To improve
Reaction of your employee • Were they receptive or defensive? • Did they express their views? • Did they come up with solutions?		
Progress • Have you been following the progress? • Do you think the feedback was useful?		

EXERCISE 3

After receiving feedback, analyse your behaviour by completing the table below:

	Analysis	To improve
Were you receptive and open-minded?		
Were you defensive? Why?		
Did you listen closely? Did you understand the message?		
In your opinion, what was the objective of the feedback? Did you understand it? Did your manager explain it clearly?		
Did you ask for clarification on the situation?		
Did you offer points for improvement? Have you put them in place?		
Did the feedback end on a positive note? If yes, what was the conclusion?		

We want to hear from you!
Leave a comment on your online library
and share your favourite books on social media!

FURTHER READING

BIBLIOGRAPHY

- Audibert, O. (2009) La pyramide des besoins de Maslow. *Psychologue du travail*. [Online]. [Accessed 30 July 2015]. Available from: <http://www.psychologue-dutravail.com/psychologie-du-travail/la-pyramide-des-besoins-de-maslow/>

- (No date) Définition : Fenêtre de Johari de Luft Ingham. *Le Dico du Marketing*. [Online]. [Accessed 14 February 2018]. Available from: <http://www.ledicodumarketing.fr/definitions/fenetre-de-johari-de-luft-ingham.html>

- (No date) Feedback. Merriam-Webster Learner's Dictionary. [Online]. [Accessed 25 August 2015]. Available from: <http://www.learnersdictionary.com/definition/feedback>

- (No date) Feed-back. *Larousse.fr*. [Online]. [Accessed 25 August 2015]. Available from: <http://www.larousse.fr/dictionnaires/francais/feed-back/33157>

- Noyé, D. (2012) *Donner et recevoir du feed-back : la reconnaissance, le recadrage*. Paris: Julhiet Éditions.

- Stone, D. and Heen, S. (2014) *Thanks for the*

Feedback: The Science and Art of Receiving Feedback Well. New York: Penguin.

- Whitmore, J. (2017) *Coaching for Performance: The Principles and Practice of Coaching and Leadership.* Boston, Massachusetts: Nicholas Brealey Publishing.

50MINUTES.com

www.50minutes.com

Ebook EAN: 9782806279392

Paperback EAN: 9782806286130

Legal Deposit: D/2016/12603/549

Cover: © Primento

Digital conception by Primento, the digital partner of publishers.